### STEP-UP Books

are written especially for children who have outgrown beginning readers. In this exciting series:

- the words are harder (but not too hard)
- there's more text (but it's still in big print)
- there are plenty of illustrations (but the books aren't picture books)
- the subject matter has been carefully chosen to appeal to young readers who want to find out about the world around them. They'll love these informative and lively books.

### PUT YOUR FOOT IN YOUR MOUTH
### and other silly sayings

Did you know that the expression
- "come to a head" started with cabbages
- "stick your neck out" started with chickens
- "have a skeleton in the closet" started with doctors?

This humorously illustrated, carefully researched book reveals how we came to use certain everyday expressions and what they really mean.

# Put Your Foot in Your Mouth

## and other silly sayings

by James A. Cox

illustrated by
Sam Q. Weissman

Step-Up Books · Random House
New York

Copyright © 1980 by Random House, Inc.
All rights reserved under International and Pan-American Copyright Conventions. Published in the United States by Random House, Inc., New York, and simultaneously in Canada by Random House of Canada Limited, Toronto.

*Library of Congress Cataloging in Publication Data:*
Cox, James A. Put your foot in your mouth and other silly sayings. (Step-up-books; 31) SUMMARY: Discusses the origin and meaning of 21 sayings used in American English.   1. English language—Terms and phrases—Juvenile literature.   2. English language—Etymology—Juvenile literature.   [1. English   language—Terms   and   phrases.   2. English   language—Etymology]   I. Weissman, Sam Q.   II. Title.   PE1574.C6   422   80-12877   ISBN: 0-394-84503-X (trade);   0-394-94503-4 (lib. bdg.)

Manufactured in the United States of America       1 2 3 4 5 6 7 8 9 0

# Contents

# People Say the Siliest Things

Did your mother ever warn you not to bite off more than you can chew? Did your teacher ever tell you to put your shoulder to the wheel? Did your father ever tell you that you are getting too big for your britches? Sometimes people say the silliest things!

But these sayings are not really silly. They all mean something. They are called idioms (ID-ee-umz). Idioms are like word pictures. They help to make the way we talk more interesting. And they help other people understand what we are talking about.

There are hundreds of idioms in the English language. Many of them are very old. But some of them are not much older than you are. Most people use idioms every day when they talk. They use idioms without thinking about them. They don't know how these sayings got started. And sometimes they are not even sure what the sayings mean.

That is what this book is about. It will tell about some idioms. About how they got started. And what they mean. Happy reading!

# Pay Through the Nose

Did you ever pay too much for something? If you did, you "paid through the nose."

No one seems to know for sure how this saying got started. But an Irish legend may be the answer. It is about 1,200 years old.

Way back then, Ireland was ruled by the Vikings. The Vikings were pirates from Northern Europe. They came to Ireland in ships. They made war on the Irish farmers. They beat the farmers and took their land.

Then they demanded a lot of money and gifts from the Irish. If an Irishman did not pay, the Vikings punished him. They slit his nose with a sharp sword.

The Irish did not want to give their money to the Vikings. But they did not want to get a slit nose, either. So they paid. But they said they "paid through the nose."

# Left Holding the Bag

If you are "left holding the bag," you have to take all the blame for something.

This is an American saying. It probably started in the early 1800s. It comes from a trick that country boys played on city boys.

Suppose a city boy was visiting his aunt in the country. The country boys would invite him to go hunting for birds called snipe.

Picture this. It is a dark night. The boys go on the snipe hunt. The country boys lead the city boy far into the woods. He does not know that snipe don't live in woods. The boys give him a lantern and a big bag. They tell him to do two things. First, hold the bag open. Second, hold the lantern above it. They will go deeper into the woods, they say. They will chase the snipe out of their nests. The birds will be scared. They will run toward his light. And they will jump right into his bag.

But that is not what happens. The country boys sneak out of the woods. They go home to bed. They leave the city boy alone in the dark forest. They leave him waiting for birds that do not even live in the woods. They leave him standing there, holding a bag open. The next day they all laugh. They ask the city boy how many snipe jumped into his bag.

"To be left holding the bag" became an idiom. We use it when one person has to take all the blame. Other people were supposed to share the blame. But they sneaked away, like the country boys. They left the one person "holding the bag."

We use the phrase another way. Suppose a bunch of people agree to do something. But only one person shows up. The others have backed out of doing the job. One poor person is "left holding the bag."

# Bite Off More Than You Can Chew

When do you "bite off more than you can chew"? When you try to do more than you really can.

What happens if you take a great big bite of cake? Your mouth is so full, you can hardly chew. And your mother says, "Don't bite off more than you can chew."

That's good advice for other things, too. Maybe you are a busy person. You deliver newspapers every morning. You go to school all day. You join the scouts or the 4-H Club. You play on a Little League team. You collect stamps. You take dancing lessons. Or guitar lessons. Or gymnastics. Or karate (kuh-RAH-tee). And then somebody asks you to play the bass drum in the school band. If you say yes, you will be "biting off more than you can chew." You don't have time to do everything.

This saying started in America about 100 years ago. In those days, many men chewed tobacco. The tobacco was pressed into a solid block. It looked like a chocolate bar. But it didn't taste like chocolate! This bar was called a "plug." A bite of it was called a "chew." Most men said "chaw" instead of "chew."

Sometimes a man would offer another man a chaw of his tobacco plug. If the second man was greedy, he would take a big bite. If the chaw was too big, he would have trouble chewing it. He would start to choke on it. He would swallow tobacco juice and get sick.

Then the first man would laugh. He would say, "Serves you right for biting off more than you can chew."

# In Hot Water

If you are "in hot water," you are in trouble. You are like someone stewing in a cannibal's big pot.

This idiom may have started many hundreds of years ago. At that time, there were no policemen. People had to protect themselves from robbers. Sometimes a robber tried to break into a house. The people inside wanted to chase him away. So they dumped a kettle of boiling water on him. That hot water meant trouble for the robber!

Or the saying may have started another way. Today, we have law courts. Trials are held in the courts. Judges and juries decide whether people have broken the law. They decide whether people are guilty (GILL-tee) or innocent (IN-uh-sent). Guilty means that they did break the law. Innocent means that they did not.

Hundreds of years ago, there were no courts. People were judged innocent or guilty by cruel tests. The tests were called "trial by ordeal." There were many kinds of ordeals. In one, people had to stick their hands into a pot of boiling water. They had to pick up a ring from the bottom of the pot. If the boiling water did not hurt them, they were innocent. But if the boiling water did hurt them, they were guilty. The idea was to let God be the judge. God was not supposed to let innocent people be harmed.

The test was painful and unfair. People could not pass it. They were burned even if they were innocent. So they tried very hard to stay out of trouble. They didn't want to get in hot water.

# Cut Off Your Nose to Spite Your Face

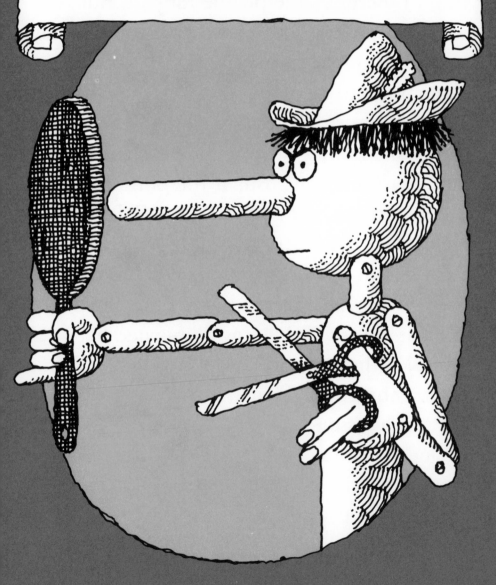

Suppose some of your friends borrow your bike. And then they smash it up. Would you forgive them? Some people forgive. But other people do not. They are spiteful. They want to pay back someone who harms them. They want to hurt that person. And they are willing to hurt themselves to do it. So we say they are "cutting off their nose to spite their face."

This phrase comes from France. In 1593 Henry IV (the Fourth) was the king of France. But a lot of French people didn't want Henry to be their king. The whole city of Paris was against him. Paris was the capital of France. So Henry decided to make war on the city. "That will teach the people of Paris a lesson," he said.

One of his men argued with him. "You want to be the king of the people of Paris," he said. "You want that beautiful city to be your capital. But what good is the city if your guns wreck it? What good are the people if you kill them all? You would be the king of a dead city. That would be like cutting off your nose to spite your face. Would you chop off your nose to teach your face a lesson?"

Henry thought about it. He decided that the man was right. So he spared the city of Paris and its people. Henry really was a good man. And after a while he became the most popular king France ever had.

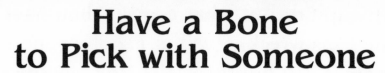

# Have a Bone to Pick with Someone

If you "have a bone to pick," you have something to argue about. Or else you are not happy about what somebody is doing. Here is an example. "The teacher had a bone to pick with Karen. Karen forgot to do her homework for three nights in a row."

This saying comes from England. It probably started in the 1500s. When people disagreed, they thought of dogs fighting over a bone. So they called the thing they disagreed about a "bone." Why did they use the word "pick"? At that time, "to pick" meant to look for a fight. So they said, "I have a bone to pick with you."

# Spill the Beans

Did anyone ever tell you a secret? You were not supposed to tell anyone else. But you did. That is called "spilling the beans."

Suppose it is Marty's birthday. His mother decides to have a surprise party for him. Some of the kids tell Marty about the party ahead of time. They are "spilling the beans."

This phrase has a long history. Two or three thousand years ago, the Greeks had secret clubs. Only special people could be members. When someone wanted to join, the club members took a vote. It was a secret vote. The club members voted with beans. Each one put a bean in the same jar. A white bean was a "yes" vote. It meant that the person could join the club. A brown bean was a "no" vote.

The leaders of the club counted the beans in the jar. If all of them were white, the person was allowed to join. But if a few beans were brown, the person could not be a member.

Of course, most of the beans might be brown. Or all of them might be brown. That's one reason the vote was kept secret. No one likes to find out that everyone voted against him. That hurts!

But sometimes a clumsy voter would knock the jar over. The beans would spill out. And everyone would see how many were white and how many were brown. The vote would not be secret anymore.

The Greeks turned this into a saying. They used it when someone told a secret of any kind. They said that person had "spilled the beans." And we still use this old Greek saying today.

# Blow Your Own Horn

Some people brag. They talk big. They boast about things they can do. These people make a lot of noise about themselves. They don't wait for someone else to pay attention to them. They "blow their own horn" to get attention.

"Blow your own horn" is an old saying. It started in England with a man named Fleming. He wrote a book in 1576. In the book he said, "I will sound the trumpet of mine owne merites." Does that look like it is spelled wrong? It isn't. Spelling has changed a lot in 400 years.

What Fleming said means, "I will blow my own horn." (A trumpet is one kind of horn.) He did blow his own horn. And so do many people today.

# In One Ear and Out the Other

When does something go "in one ear and out the other"? When you hear something but don't really pay attention.

You listen with your ears. But it is your mind that makes sense of the words you hear. At times your mind is not paying attention. Then the words don't mean a thing. It is as if the words went into your head through one ear. But your brain didn't catch them. So they went right out through the other ear.

Sometimes children in school get bored. They don't really listen to the teacher. They

are thinking of something else. What the teacher is saying goes in one ear and out the other. Then the teacher calls someone's name. And the pupil does not even know what the question was!

Sometimes grownups also have trouble paying attention. "In one ear . . ." was first used in England in the 1500s. A famous minister gave a talk in a church. Everyone there thought his talk was boring. One person said that the minister's words almost put him to sleep. He said they went "in at the one eare and out at the other."

# Stick Your Neck Out

If you "stick your neck out," you are taking a foolish chance.

A hundred years ago cities were not as big as they are today. Many people lived on farms and in small villages. They raised their own pigs and chickens.

When a mother decided to have chicken for Sunday dinner, she called to her children. "Bring me a plump bird," she told them.

The children would catch the chicken. They would take it to a chopping block. The chopping block usually was a tree stump. They would chop off the chicken's head with an ax.

Maybe you have never been on a farm. Maybe you have only seen chickens in plastic bags in the supermarket. You may not like the idea of chopping off a chicken's head. But if you want to eat roast chicken, someone has to do the job.

Many years ago most people did it themselves. They did it so often they got used to it. In fact, they had a slang saying. When something bad happened to a person, they would say, "Old Charlie got it in the neck." Or they would say, "Charlie got it where the chicken got the ax."

After a while, another saying grew out of this old one. A chicken on the chopping block usually stretched its neck out. The chicken seemed to be giving the person with the ax a good target to swing at. The chicken wasn't, of course. It was scared. It was trying to get away.

But the chicken seemed to be sticking its neck out for the ax. People remembered that when someone took a very risky chance. "Charlie is doing something foolish," they would say. "He's almost asking to get killed. He's really sticking his neck out."

# Too Big for Your Britches

Has anyone ever said you were "too big for your britches"? That means you were too proud of yourself.

Maybe you began to feel very important. You acted as if you knew more than you really did. You started getting bossy. You even told your parents what to do.

Your mom and dad didn't like that, of course. "We understand that you are growing up," they may have said. "But you are not as grown-up as you think!" Your parents thought you were trying to grow up too fast. If you grew that fast, you would grow right out of your clothes!

In the 1600s, people said a bossy young person was "too big for his boots."

In the 1700s, he was "too big for his breeches." What were breeches? They were pants that came to the knee. Sometimes they had silver buckles on them.

In the 1800s, men and boys wore long pants. In America, long pants were called "britches" instead of breeches. People said a young person acting too important was "too big for his britches."

Today we have the word "swellhead." People who are swellheads are also very proud of themselves. Their heads are swollen. In fact, their heads are too big for their hats.

Anybody can be a swellhead. Young people can be swellheads. So can grownups.

But we never say that grownups are getting "too big for their britches." We let only young people do that!

# Paddle Your Own Canoe

Suppose your aunt says to you, "Go paddle your own canoe." She is telling you to mind your own business. Now suppose she says, "My friend Sue has been paddling her own canoe since she was a girl." Your aunt means something else. She means that Sue has been taking care of herself.

This saying probably started in the 1800s. In 1854 it was used in a song. The song was in a magazine called *Harper's Monthly*. Part of the song went like this:

> Voyager upon life's seas,
> To yourself be true.
> And whate'er your lot may be,
> Paddle your own canoe.

President Lincoln liked the saying very much. He used it often. Because he was famous, people copied him. That is how the idiom became popular. And it still is.

# Have Your Heart in the Right Place

If you want to do the right thing, you "have your heart in the right place."

Where is your heart? It is inside your chest, between your lungs. But it is not in the middle. It lies just a bit to the left.

For hundreds of years, most people did not know this. They were not sure where the heart was. Some people even thought it moved around inside the body. Sometimes they were nervous or excited. They felt their hearts beating in their throats. They said their hearts were in their mouths.

Sometimes people got scared. They said they could feel their hearts fall. This led to some silly sayings. One man said that he was so afraid, his heart fell into his toe. Another man said he felt his heart fall into his heel. Much later, someone said his heart was in his boots. Today, some people say, "My heart fell into my shoes." Or, "My heart dropped."

And today we still use another old saying about the heart. We use it about people who let everyone know their most secret feelings. We say they are wearing their hearts on their sleeves. One of the first people to talk about hearts on sleeves was William Shakespeare (SHAKE-speer). He was a very famous writer. He was born in 1564 and died in 1616.

By Shakespeare's time, most people knew where the heart was. They knew that it didn't really jump into their throats. It didn't drop into their toes either. They knew there was a right place for the heart. So they made up another idiom. It was about people who try hard to do the right thing. You might hear your Uncle Bill say something like this, "Sometimes Joe seems like an old crab. But he means well. His heart is in the right place."

# Like Greased Lightning

What is faster than Superman? Greased lightning. When you say something is "like greased lightning," you mean it is faster than the fastest thing you can think of.

This saying started in the 1800s. People sometimes wanted to talk about something that was super fast. They thought of the fastest thing they knew: lightning. (They had never heard of Superman.)

Lightning is a flash of light. It travels at the speed of 186,000 miles a second. That's fast! But **greased** lightning would be even faster. Why? Well, people greased wagon wheels. That made the wheels turn faster. So why not grease the lightning to make **it** faster?

Of course, they could not really grease the lightning. But they could pretend. They could say that something was as fast as "greased lightning."

This is known as exaggerating
(ig-ZAJ-uh-rate-ing). That means saying
that something is better—or faster—than it
really is. We all exaggerate sometimes. We
may do it to show off. But it doesn't work
very often.

I would be exaggerating if I said it did.

# Come to a Head

When things "come to a head," something is ready to happen.

This idiom started with a cabbage. There are many kinds of cabbage. The one we know best is green, round, and hard. Its leaves are wrapped tightly around each other. This cabbage looks something like a person's head. In fact, we usually talk about a **head** of cabbage. The word "cabbage" comes from an old Latin word. The Latin word means head.

But a cabbage plant does not always look like a head. When it is young, its leaves are loose. The leaves look like the petals of a big, green flower. Then the cabbage starts to get ripe. The inside leaves wrap tightly around each other. They form a hard, green ball. That's when the cabbage starts to look like a head.

In the 1400s cabbage was the main food for poor people in England. But in some years the cabbages took a long time to get ripe.

So the housewives would go to the farmer. "Our children are hungry," they would say. "Where are the cabbages?"

And the farmer would answer, "I am sorry about your children. But the cabbages are not ripe yet. You will just have to wait until they come to a head."

Today we use that same phrase. We use it to talk about something that is ready to happen. Suppose your family plans to move far away. You are very excited. But before you go, your parents have to find a new house. They have to sell the old house. They have many other things to do. But you want to know **when** you are going to move. "We will know soon," your mother says at last. "Things are coming to a head."

# Lead by the Nose

When you "lead someone by the nose," you make that person do anything you want.

People first tamed animals about 8,000 years ago. They kept cattle—cows and oxen—in herds. They needed the cattle for milk and meat. From the skin of the cows they made leather. They also used cattle as work animals. Cows and oxen carried heavy loads. They pulled plows and carts, too.

How did early people steer their work animals? They put a metal ring through each animal's nose. Then they tied a piece of rope to the ring. In that way, a person could lead the animal. It would go wherever it was led.

Why did people put the ring through the animal's nose? Because noses are very sensitive. If you bump your nose, it hurts a lot. The pain makes you want to cry. Animals feel the same way. When someone pulled a cow's nose ring, its nose hurt. The cow soon learned to obey.

The first person to talk about leading people by the nose was Isaiah (aye-ZAY-uh). Things he said are written in the Bible. Isaiah used the idiom almost 3,000 years ago. Some sayings sure do last a long time!

# Have a Skeleton in the Closet

Do you "have a skeleton in your closet"? Yes? Then you are hiding something you are ashamed of.

Everybody knows what a skeleton is. It is a group of bones strung together. It looks like a person with no skin or flesh. Skeletons make good Halloween decorations. And sometimes we see them in scary movies.

But skeletons are important in other ways. If you want to become a doctor, you will have to go to medical school. You will have to learn how bodies work. Skeletons will help you—real skeletons. A real skeleton is made of the bones of a real person.

Two thousand years ago, doctors did not study the bodies of people very much. They were afraid to dissect (dye-SEKT)—cut up—a dead person. They were afraid the ghost of the dead person would haunt them.

A few hundred years ago, doctors were not afraid anymore. They did not believe in ghosts. They wanted to cut up dead bodies to learn more. But now there were laws. The laws said that doctors could not dissect just any dead person. They could dissect only the bodies of dead criminals.

But there weren't enough dead criminals for all the doctors. So men called "grave robbers" went to work. They would go to a cemetery at night. They would dig up the body of someone who had just died. They would sell the body to a doctor for a very high price.

Most people did not like the idea of doctors cutting up bodies. They thought that was a bad thing to do. Sometimes they beat up the doctors. Sometimes they put the doctors in jail. The doctors did not want to get into trouble. But they had to learn. So doctors would take just one chance. A doctor would cut up only one body. He would learn as much as he could from it that one time. And he would keep the skeleton. He could keep learning from it.

Where could he put the skeleton? He could not keep it where anyone would see it. That might get him into trouble. So he usually hid the skeleton in a dark closet. No one was likely to see it there. It was his secret.

But people knew that most doctors had a skeleton in their closet. After a while, "skeleton in the closet" became an idiom. It was used about a person or a family with something to hide. They had a secret they were ashamed of. They were like a doctor with a skeleton in the closet.

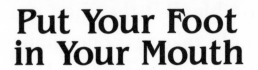

# Put Your Foot in Your Mouth

Did you ever say something stupid or silly? Did you ever blurt out something without thinking? Did your foolish words embarrass someone? If your answers are yes, you "put your foot in your mouth."

This saying probably started with an animal disease, of all things. The disease is called foot-and-mouth disease. Cattle and sheep get it. So do other animals with hoofs for feet. The disease gives them sores in their mouths and around their hoofs.

Foot-and-mouth disease is serious. But if you change just one word, the name becomes funny. It becomes foot-**in**-mouth disease.

Someone with a foot in his mouth looks pretty foolish. So a person who says something foolish could have "foot-in-mouth disease." And who would think of such a disease? An animal doctor, of course.

An animal doctor was probably the one to

change "foot-and-mouth" to "foot-in-mouth."

He might have said, "That's the trouble with old Arthur. He's got foot-in-mouth disease."

Today we might say, "Arthur sure put his foot in his mouth that time." Both sayings mean the same thing.

"To put your foot in it" is an older saying. It has been around since the United States was born. It means more than just **saying** something foolish. It means also **doing** something foolish. Like putting your foot into fresh cement. Or jumping into mud.

But one expert thinks the phrase had a funnier beginning. He says it started when most Americans lived on or near farms. Some people could not walk across a cow pasture safely. They always stepped in what the cows left behind. They really put their foot in it!

# Put Your Shoulder to the Wheel

If you "put your shoulder to the wheel," you really work hard at something.

Today we ride in powerful cars. We have paved roads and highways. Our cars can go fast. They can go up steep hills easily. But before the 1900s few people owned a car. People rode in wagons pulled by horses. Most roads were not paved. They were just clay or dirt. In the summer it rained. The rain turned the roads into sticky, goopy mud. In winter the roads froze. They were covered with ice and snow. There were no snowplows. Snow stayed on the roads until it melted.

Horses are strong animals. But they could not pull heavy wagons through deep mud. They could not pull the wagons through deep snow. Even in dry weather they needed help on steep hills. So the people in the wagons would jump out. They would get behind the wagons and push. The strongest men would put their shoulders behind the back wheels. They would push as hard as they could. They would lift the wheels out of the mud if they could. They would make the wheels turn. And that would help the horse pull the wagon.

Now people say, "put your shoulder to the wheel." They want you to try as hard as you can.

# Pull the Wool Over Someone's Eyes

To "pull the wool over someone's eyes" means to fool someone.

Many years ago, ladies and gentlemen wore wigs. They wore wigs even though their heads were not bald. Wigs were the style. Sometimes they were made of human hair. But human hair costs a lot. So most wigs were made from the hair of horses, goats, and sheep.

Sheep's hair is called wool. It is usually curly. Most wigs were made of curly hair. So some people called them "wool" as a joke. Even today, "wool" is a slang word for curly hair.

No one is sure how the phrase "pull the wool over someone's eyes" got started. But here's a good guess by an expert. Suppose a boy wanted to play a joke on his uncle. The boy would sneak up behind his uncle. He would pull the uncle's wig down over his eyes. The uncle would not be able to see.

That was just for fun. But robbers did the same thing. They did it to a gentleman walking by. They would jump out of an alley. Or they would jump from behind a tree. They would pull the gentleman's wig down over his eyes. He would not be able to see what was going on. The robbers would steal his money and run away.

Today the saying means to fool somebody. It means to stop that person from seeing the truth. Suppose Tony chips one of his mother's best dishes. He is afraid that she will be angry and punish him. So he hides the dish in the back of the cupboard. He hopes that his mother will not miss it. He is trying to "pull the wool over her eyes."

# Chew the Rag

"To chew the rag" means to have a long talk with someone. Neighbors gossiping over the backyard fence are chewing the rag. So is your sister talking to her friend on the telephone.

In the 1700s to "rag" someone meant to scold that person. "To chew the rag" meant to argue. It also meant to grumble a lot.

How did the idiom come to mean what it does today? No one knows for sure. But here is one possible answer. Sailors on wooden ships were not supposed to smoke tobacco. They might set the ships on fire. So they chewed the tobacco instead.

Many sailing-ship voyages were very long. Whaling ships stayed at sea for three years or more. Often the sailors would run out of tobacco. But they had a chewing habit. So they chewed whatever they could find. They chewed soft leather. They even chewed rags.

On a ship, the sailors lived in a room called the forecastle (FOKE-sul). When they were not working, they sat in the forecastle. Most of them did not know how to read. So as they sat there, they chewed on their pieces of rag. And they told long tales to each other. They called this "chewing the rag."

Now we use the phrase to mean having a long talk.

# ABOUT THE AUTHOR AND ILLUSTRATOR

### James A. Cox
- Has his heart in the right place: Nutley, New Jersey
- Has put his shoulder to the wheel and written six books including:

    *Slashing Blades*—a hockey novel for young readers
    *Shells: Treasures from the Sea*
- Writes like greased lightning and frequently contributes to *National Geographic World*, a magazine for young people
- But has he bitten off more than he can chew by having eight children who are getting too big for their britches?
- No, he paddles his own canoe.

### Sam Q. Weissman
- Former art director for motion-picture advertising (Warner Brothers, Paramount, 20th Century-Fox)
- Traveled throughout Europe (age 6, with mommy)
- Traveled throughout Europe (age 26, with army)
- Traveled throughout Europe (age 40+, with movie)
- Now loves to stay home and play with crayons. Getting to be expert at staying inside lines
- Most recent book:

    *An Apple to Eat or Cross the Street* (author/artist)
- Lives in New York City